PROBLEM PATROL

There are many kinds of problems.

SCHOLASTIC

LITERACY
PLACE®

Copyright acknowledgments and credits appear on page 144, which constitutes an extension of this copyright page.

Copyright © 1996 by Scholastic Inc.   All rights reserved.   Printed in the U.S.A.
ISBN 0-590-48790-6

2 3 4 5 6 7 8 9 10   23   02 01 00 99 98 97 96

2

Visit
a Veterinarian's Office

There are many kinds
of problems.

Fun Problems

Solving problems can be fun.

Everyday Problems

We solve problems every day.

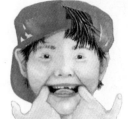

Science Problems

We use what we know to solve problems.

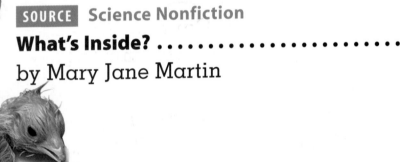

Trade Books

The following books accompany this *Problem Patrol* SourceBook.

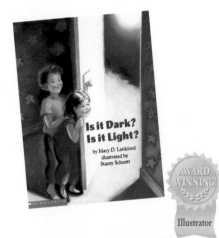

Repetitive Story
Is It Dark? Is It Light?

by Mary D. Lankford
illustrated by Stacey Schuett

Realistic Story
I Need a Lunch Box

by Jeannette Caines
illustrated by Pat Cummings

Fantasy Story
The Little Mouse, the Red Ripe Strawberry, and the Big Hungry Bear

by Don and Audrey Wood
illustrated by Don Wood

Big Books

Fiction
Across the Stream

by Mirra Ginsburg
illustrated by Nancy Tafuri

Riddle Book
It Begins With an A

by Stephanie Calmenson
illustrated by Marisabina Russo

8

Fun Problems

**Solving problems
can be fun.**

Find hidden
objects in
picture puzzles.

Meet an
elephant
who has a
hole in his
pocket. Then
sing the song
that was the
idea for
the story.

9

Who Hid It?

BY TARO GOMI

 Who hid the glove?

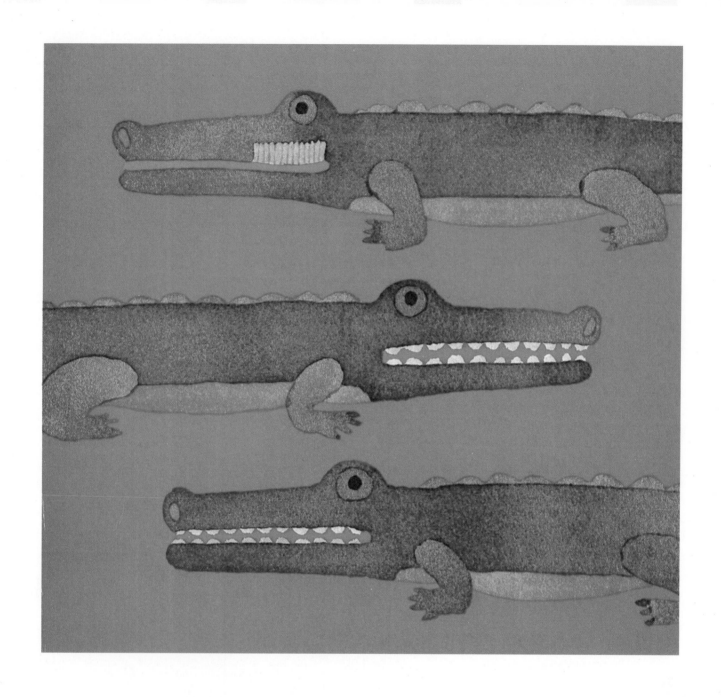

Who hid the toothbrush?

 Who hid the sock?

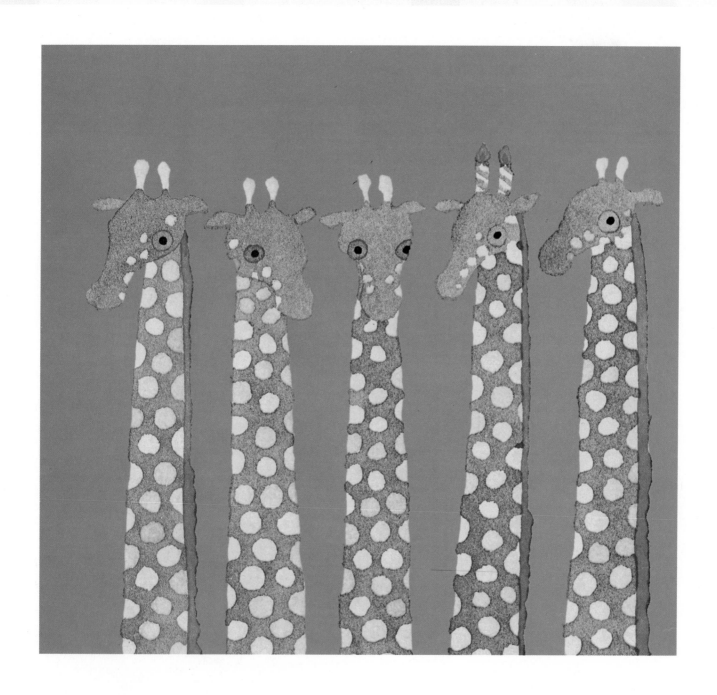

Who hid the candles?

Who hid the cap?

Who hid the magnet?

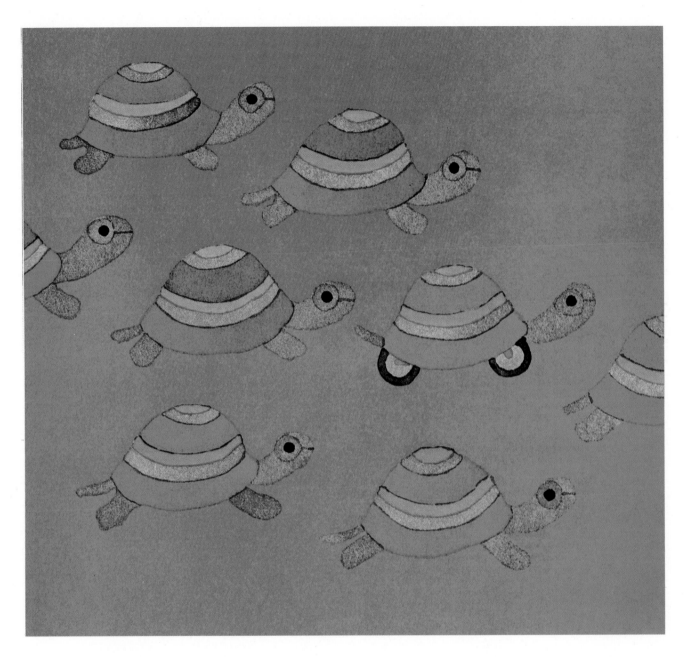

Who hid the scooter?

Who hid the flag?

18

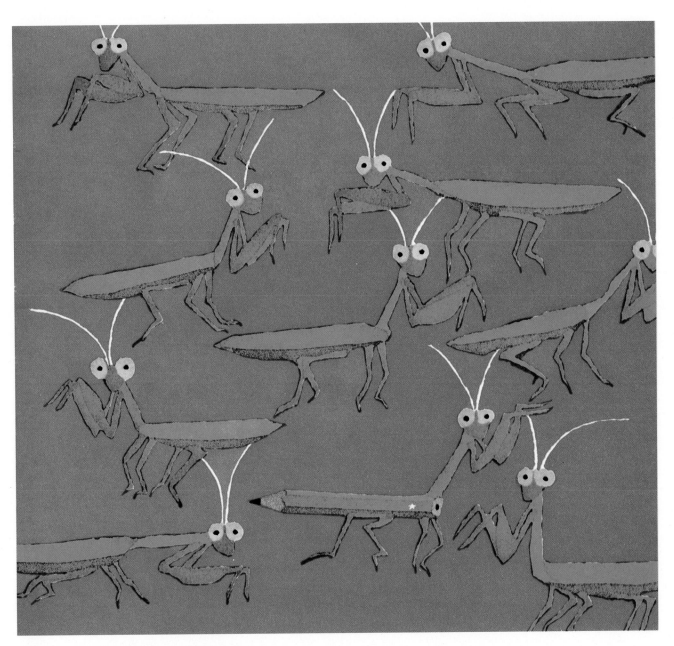

Who hid the pencils?

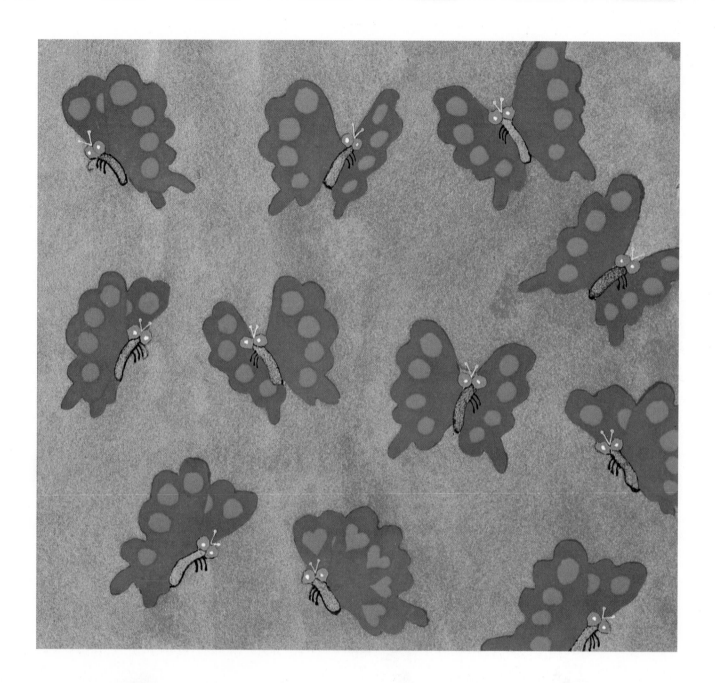

Who hid the cards?

Who hid the fork and spoon?

There's a Hole in My Pocket

Based on a Traditional American Song

Adapted by Akimi Gibson
Pictures by Jeni Bassett

SCHOLASTIC

There's a hole in my pocket.

Fix it.

How can I fix it?

Sew it.

How do I sew it?

With a needle and thread.

How can I get them?

Buy them.

How do I buy them?

With money.

Well, how can I carry it?

In your pocket.

But there's a hole in my pocket!

There's a Hole in the Bucket

SOURCE

Traditional Folk Song

 Sing Together!

HENRY SINGS:

There's a hole in the buck - et, dear Li - za, dear

Li - za. There's a hole in the buck - et, dear Li - za, a

LIZA SINGS:

hole. Well, mend it, dear Hen - ry, dear Hen - ry, dear

Hen - ry. Well, mend it, dear Hen - ry, dear Hen - ry, mend it.

Read Together!

Everyday Problems

We solve problems every day.

Follow a young boy as he looks for his missing cat.

See how a brother and sister clean up a messy room. Then read about how a boy's loose tooth falls out.

39

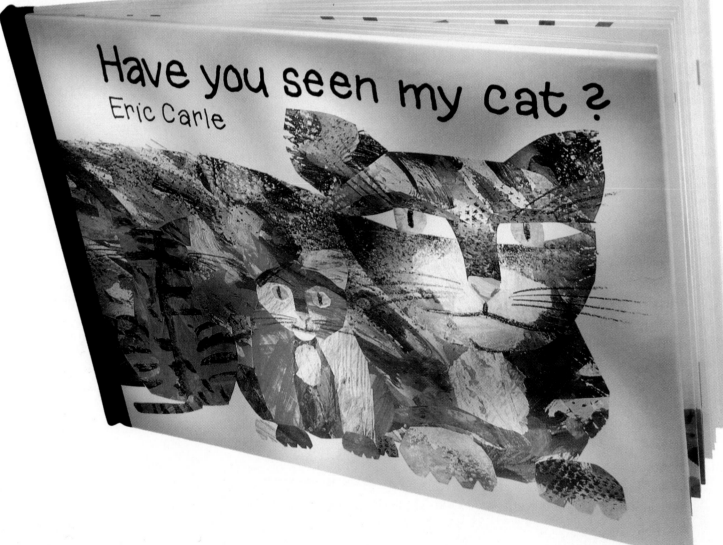

Have you seen my cat?

Eric Carle

Have you seen my cat?

This is
not
my cat!

Have you seen
my cat?

This is not my cat!

Have you seen
my cat?

This is not <u>my</u> cat!

This is not <u>my</u> cat!

Have you seen
my cat?

This is not <u>my</u> cat!

Have you seen my cat?

This is not <u>my</u> cat!

Have you seen my cat?

This is not <u>my</u> cat!

Have you seen my cat?

This is not <u>my</u> cat!

where is my cat?

Have you seen my cat?

This is my cat!

Lion

Bobcat

Panther

Tiger

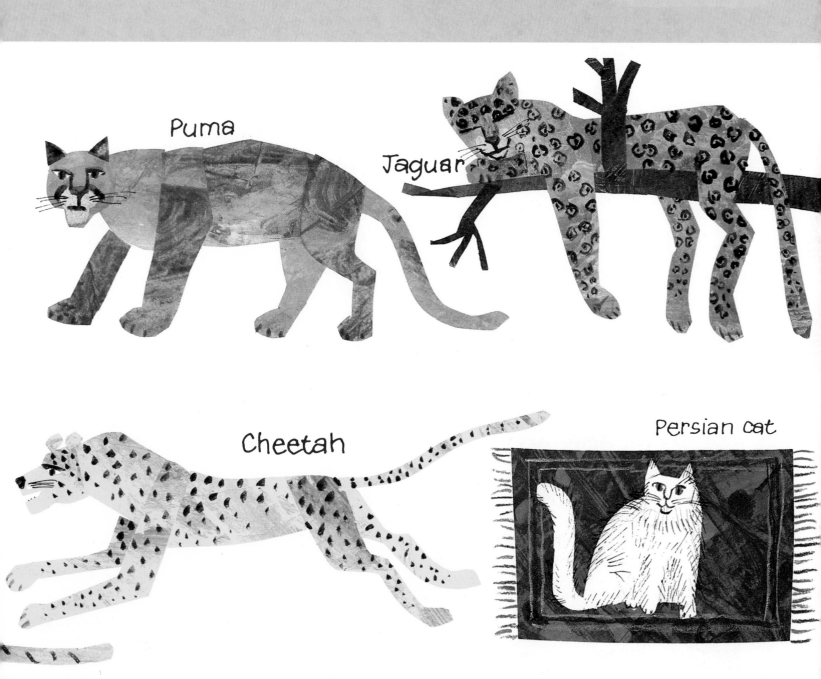

Puma

Jaguar

Cheetah

Persian cat

BET YOU CAN'T

Penny Dale

65

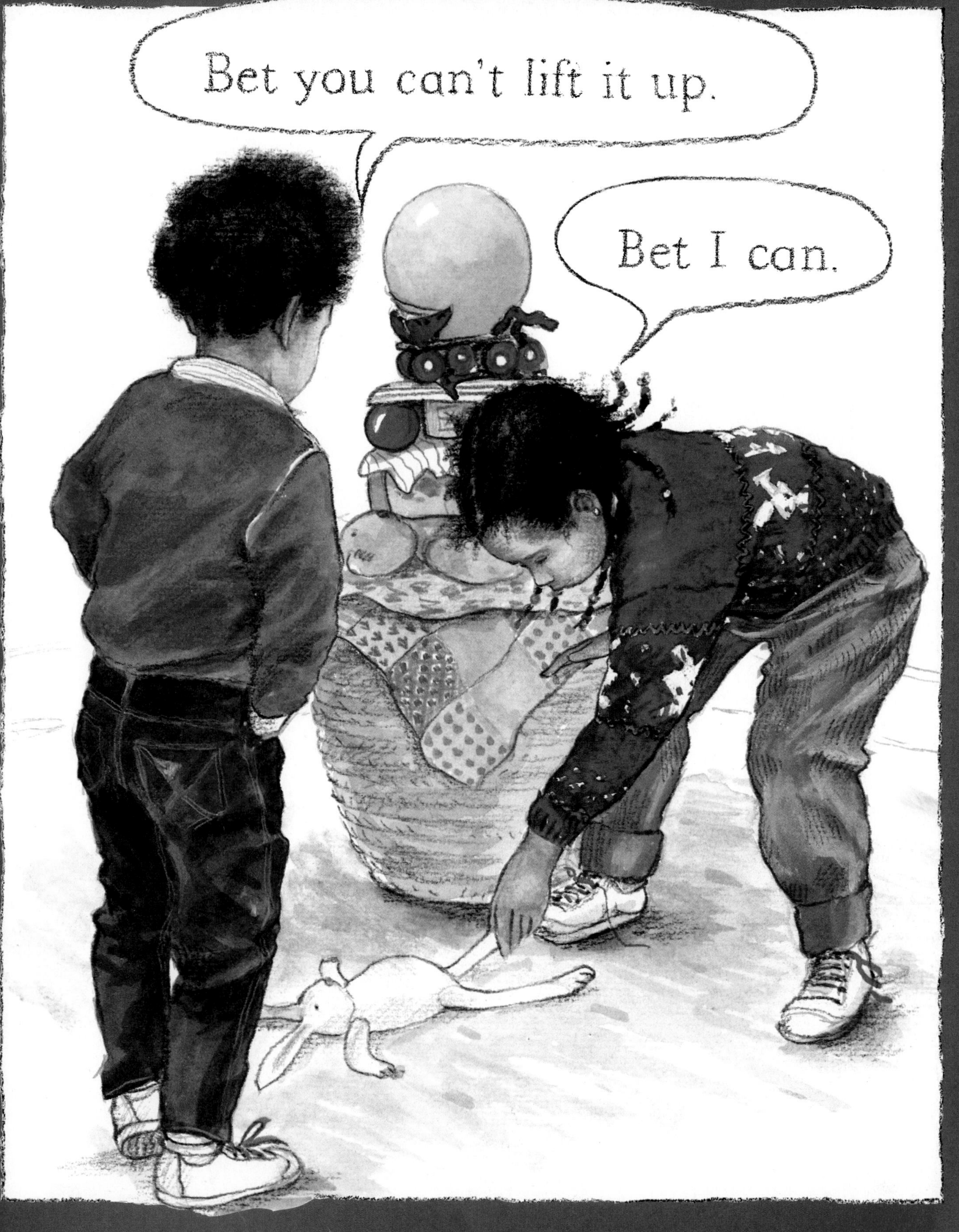
Bet you can't lift it up.
Bet I can.

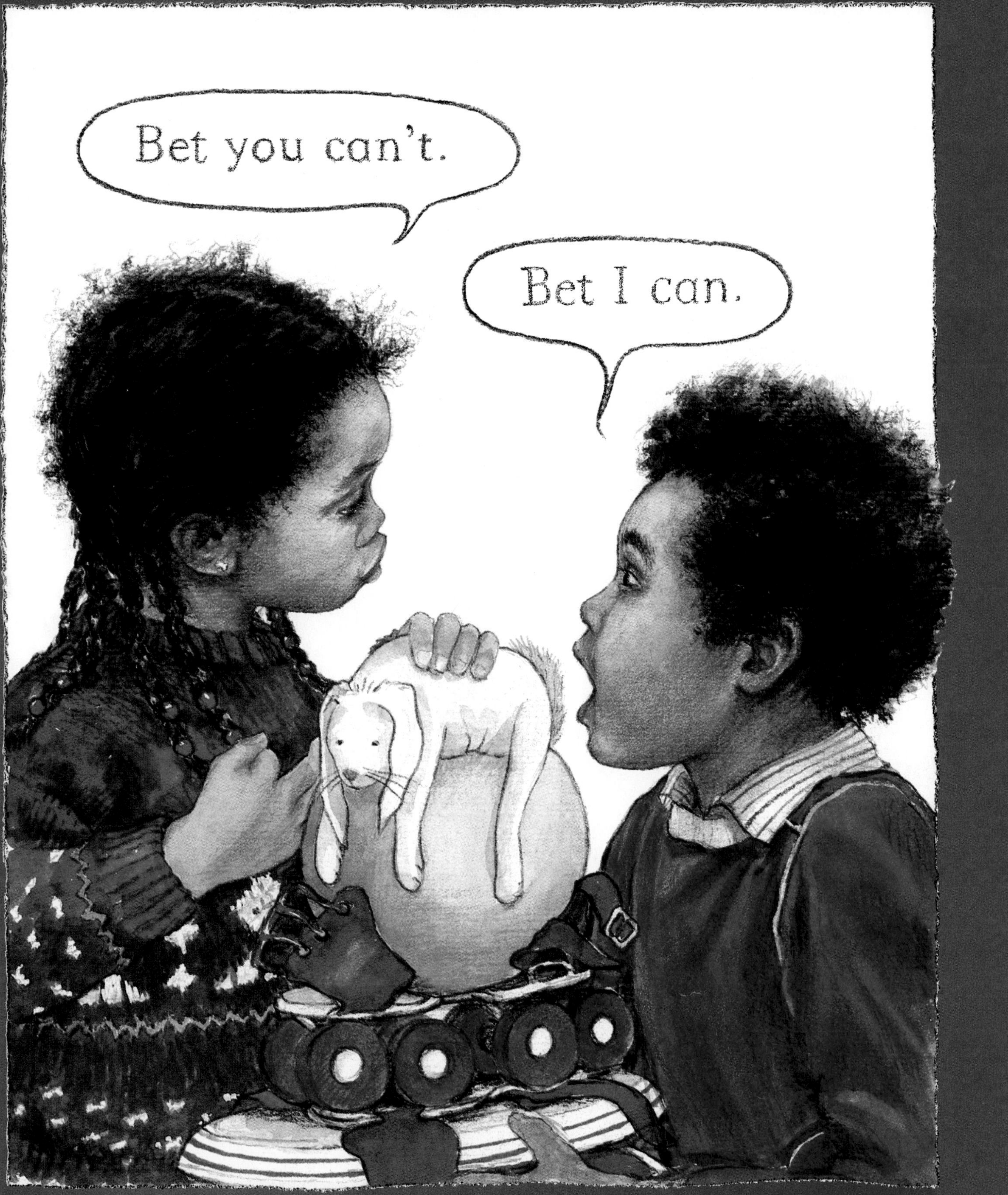
Bet you can't.
Bet I can.

80

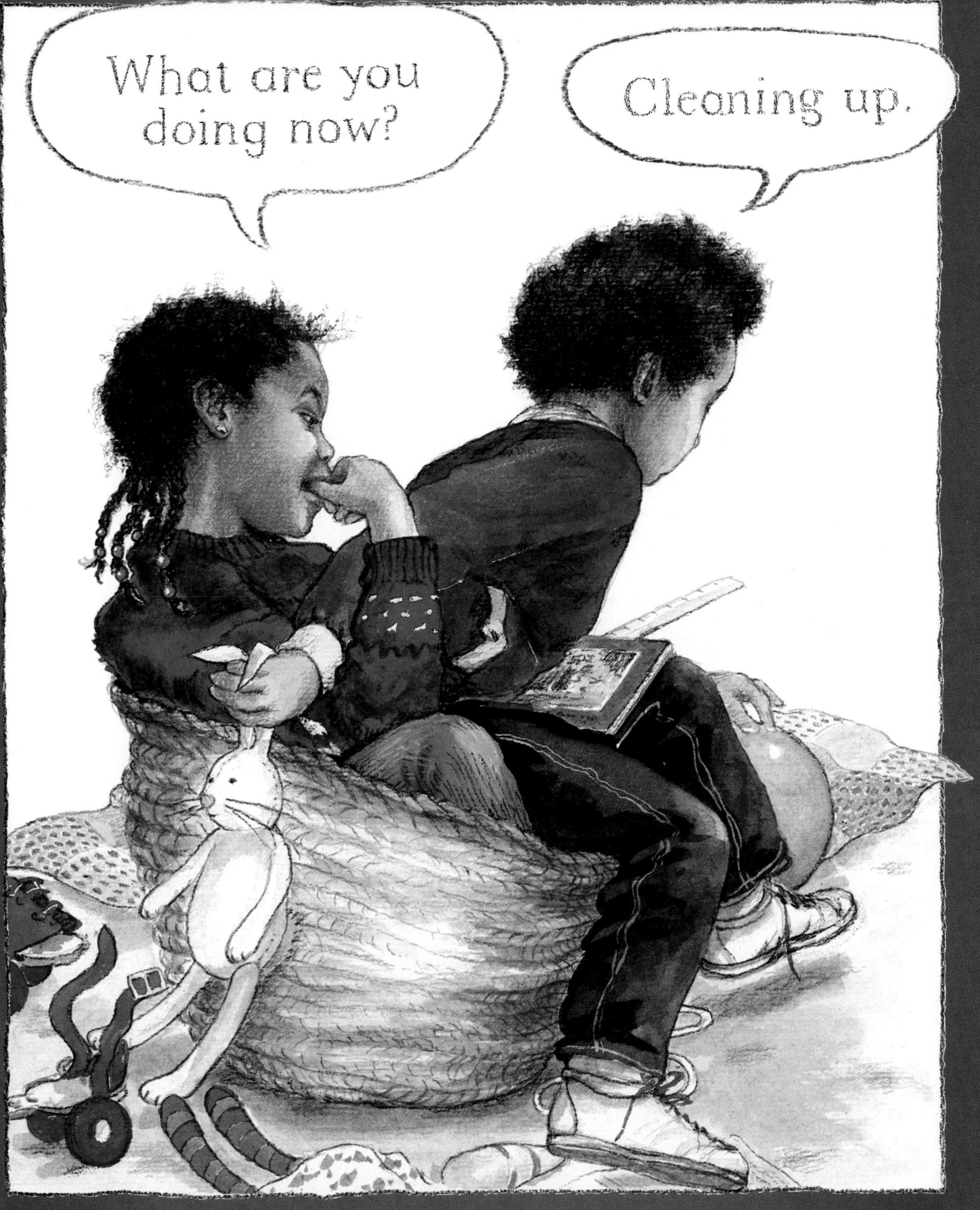
What are you doing now?
Cleaning up.

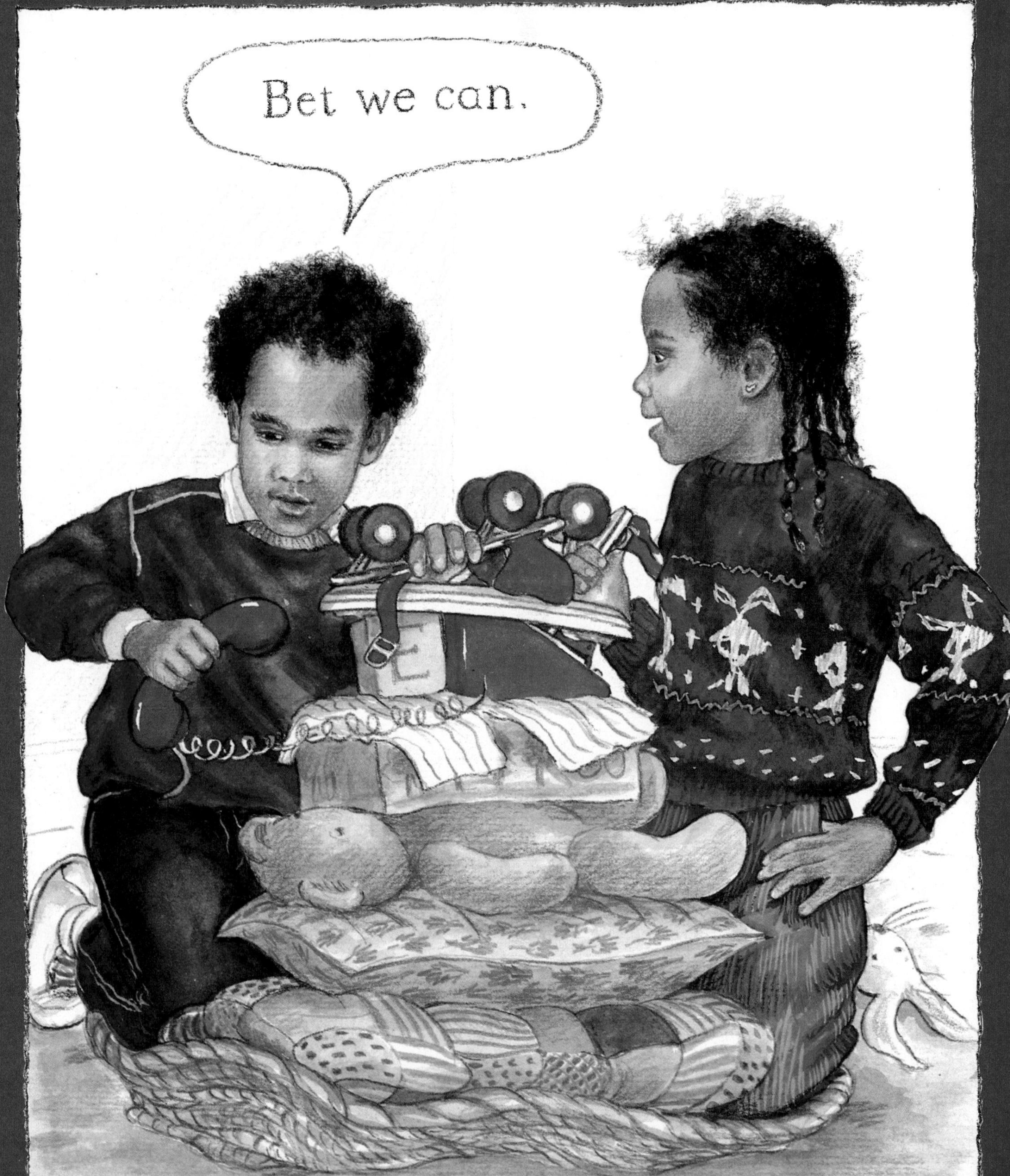
Bet we can.

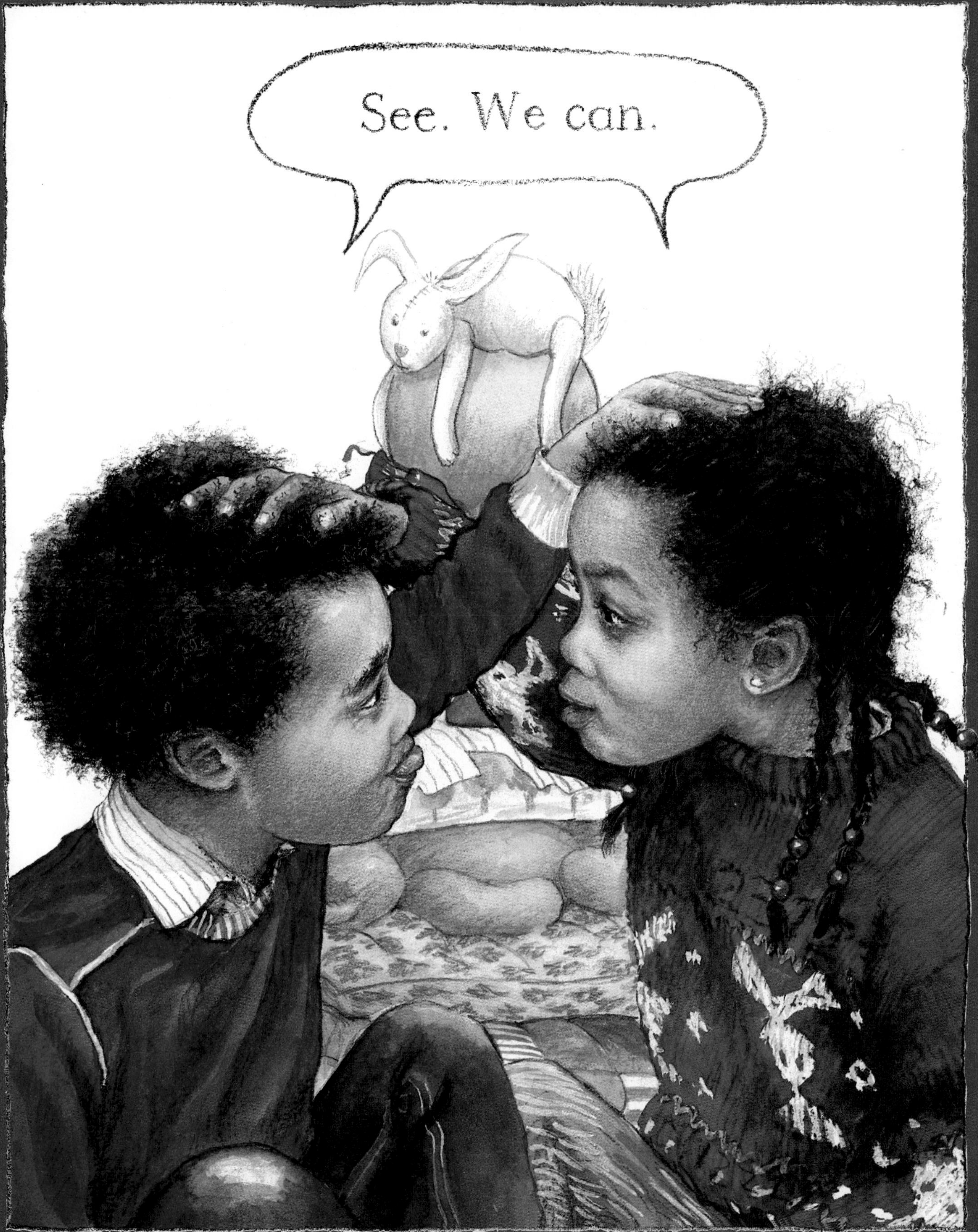
See. We can.

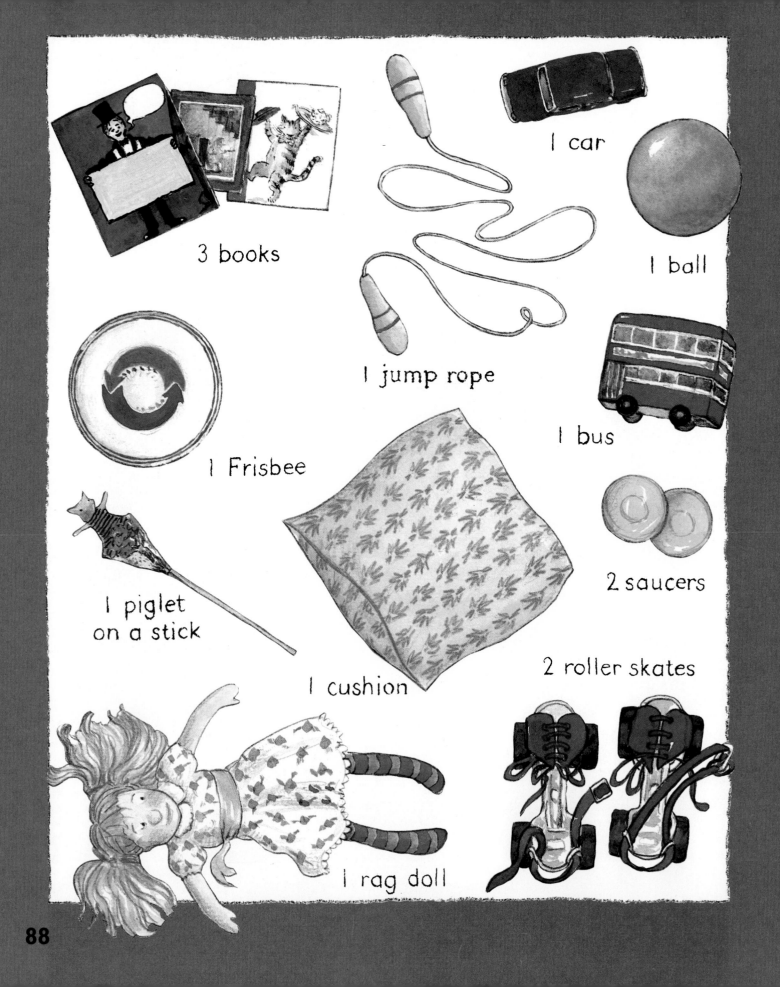

3 books

1 car

1 ball

1 jump rope

1 Frisbee

1 bus

2 saucers

1 piglet
on a stick

1 cushion

2 roller skates

1 rag doll

2 blocks

1 ruler

1 dress

1 telephone

1 yo-yo

1 rabbit

2 cups

1 quilt

1 teddy bear

1 jigsaw puzzle

1 teapot

SOURCE

Poetry Collection

Read Together!

THIS TOOTH

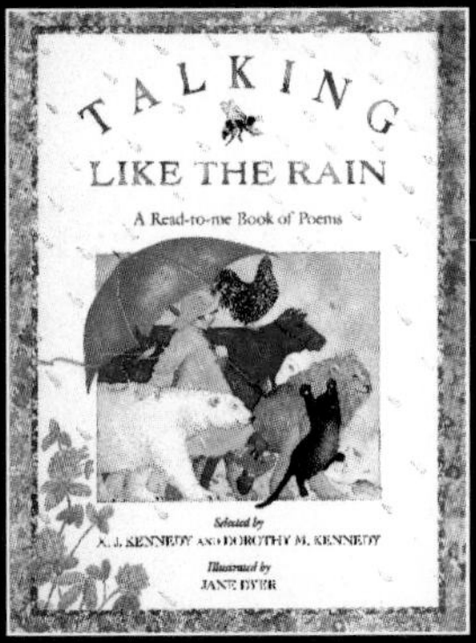

By Lee Bennett Hopkins
Illustrated by Jane Dyer

I jiggled it
    jaggled it
    jerked it.

I pushed
    and pulled
    and poked it.

But —

As soon as I stopped
and left it alone,
This tooth came out
on its very own!

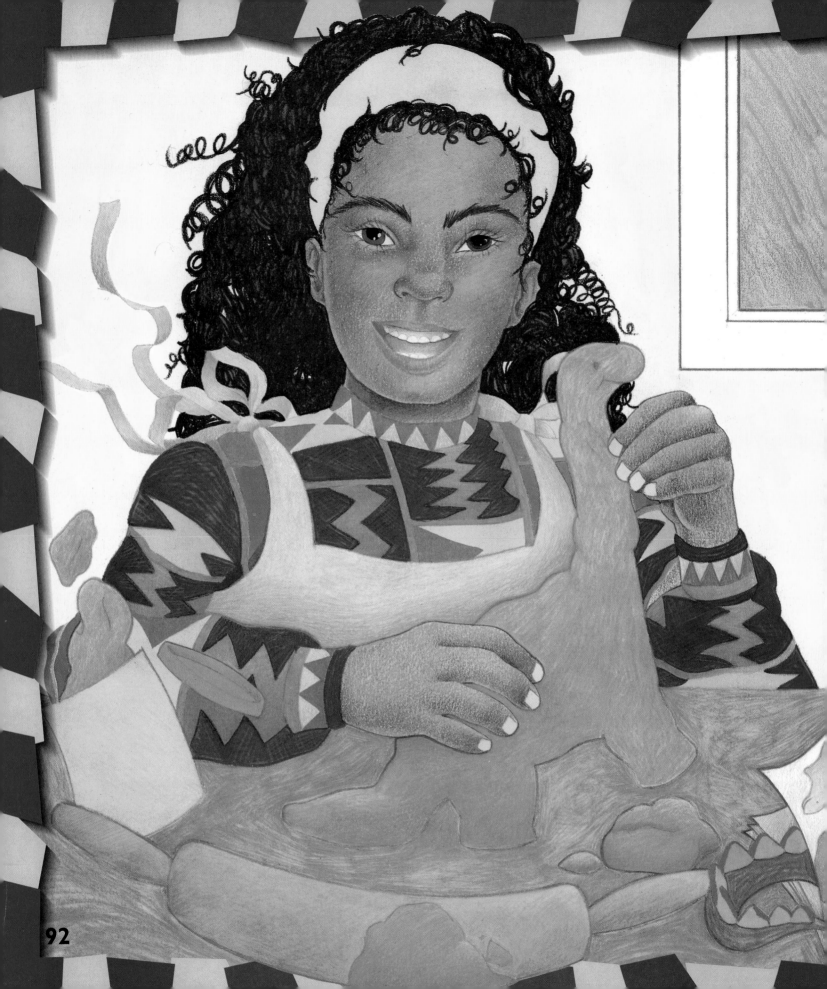

Read Together!

Science Problems

We use what we know to solve problems.

Meet a veterinarian. She solves science problems at work.

Learn about animals that hatch from eggs.

Find out how scientists dig up dinosaur bones, take them to a museum, and put them together.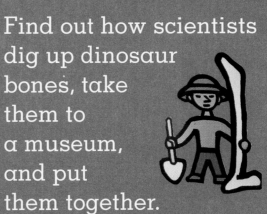

Dr. Fay Vittetoe

Veterinarian

All day long Fay Vittetoe is busy solving animal problems. See how she helps animals stay healthy.

● In the morning she gives checkups.

● In the afternoon she answers questions.

94

At the end of the day, she visits animals too big to come to her office.

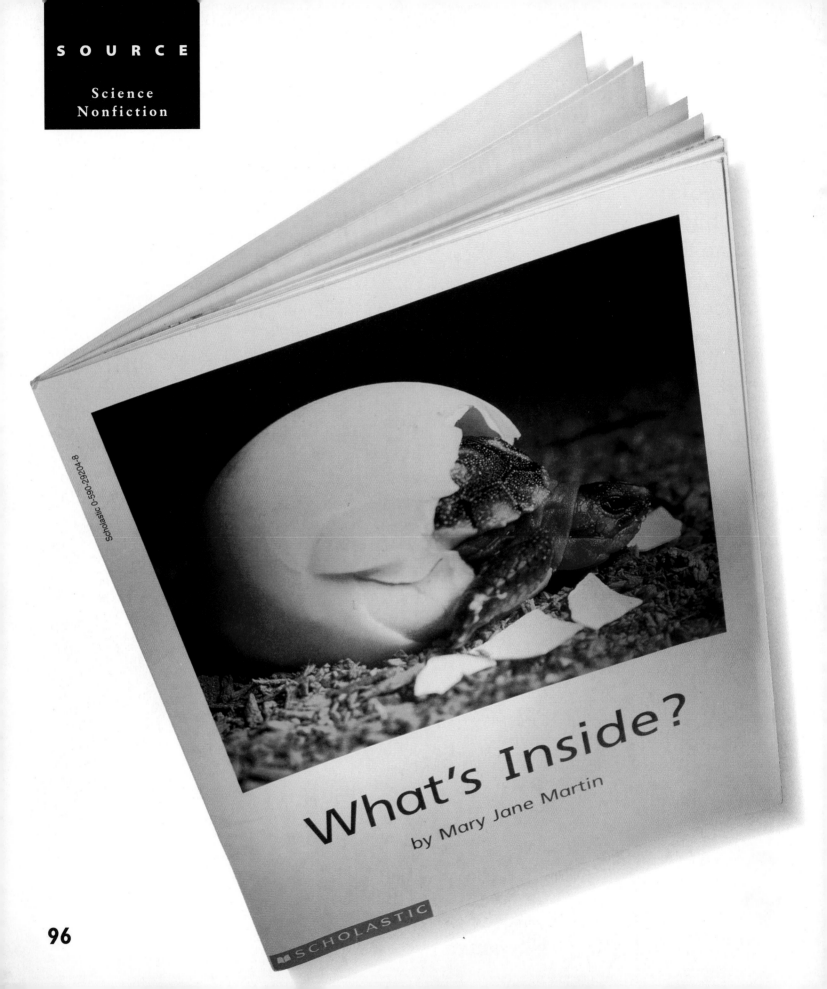

Scholastic 0-590-29204-8

What's Inside?
by Mary Jane Martin

SCHOLASTIC

What's inside?

It's a baby chicken.
That's what's inside.

What's inside?

It's a baby turtle.
That's what's inside.

What's inside?

It's a baby penguin.
That's what's inside.

What's inside?

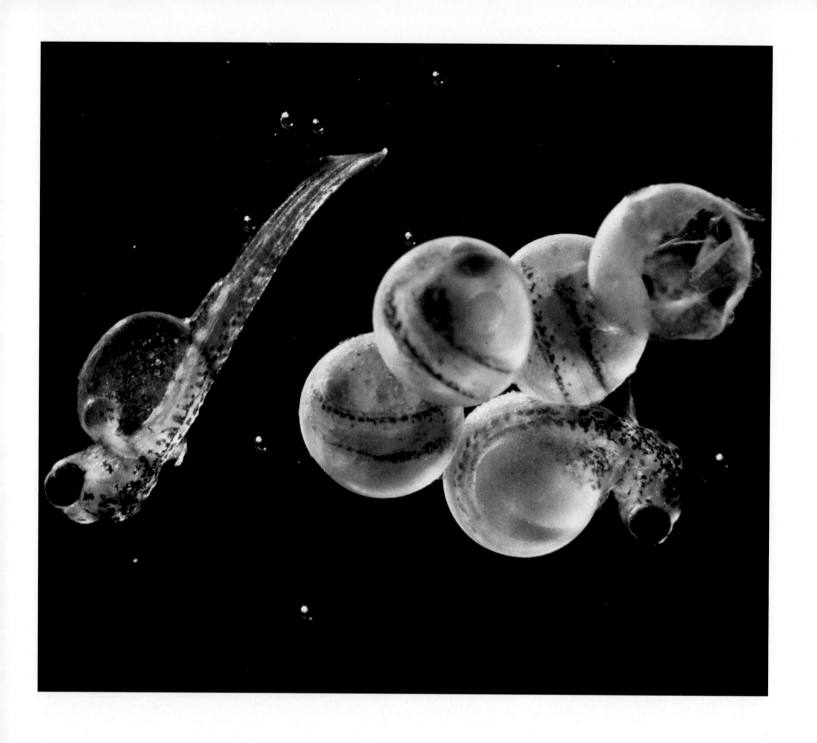

It's a baby fish.
That's what's inside.

What's inside?

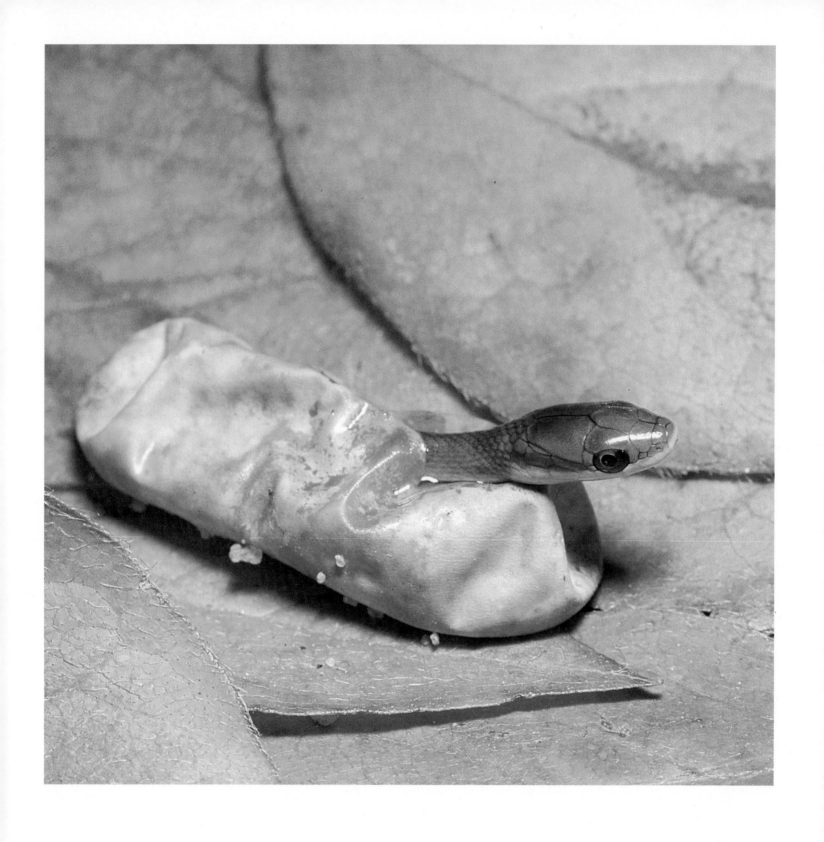

It's a baby snake.
That's what's inside.

What's inside?

It's a baby heron.
That's what's inside.

What's inside?

They're baby salamanders.
Aren't they amazing?

SOURCE

Super SCIENCE *red* ®

Magazine

AWARD WINNING Magazine

Baby Chick

By Aileen Fisher

Peck, peck, peck
on the warm brown egg.
Out comes a neck!
Out comes a leg!

How does a chick,
who's not been about,
discover the trick
of how to get out?

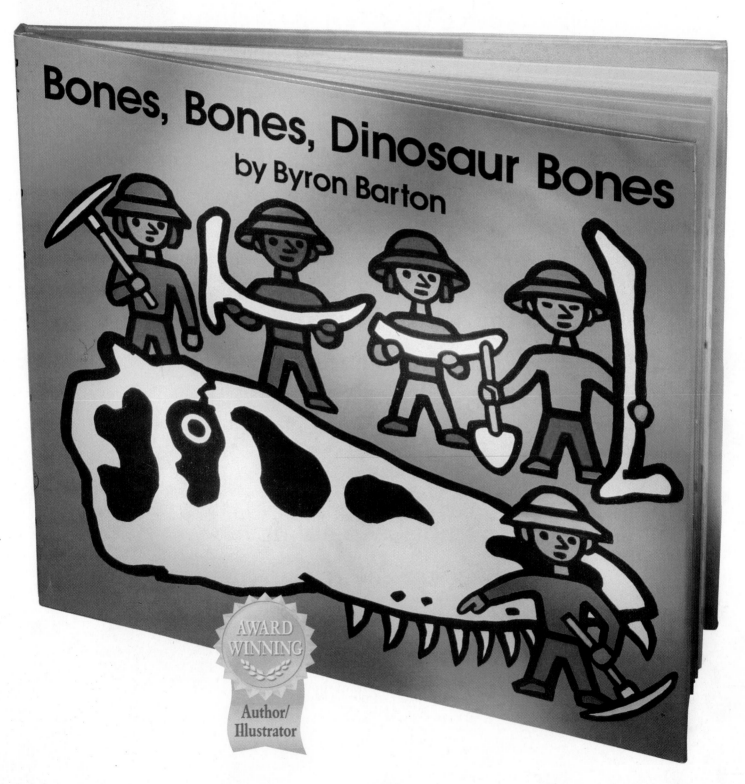

AWARD
WINNING

Author/
Illustrator

Bones. Bones. We look for bones.

Tyrannosaurus, Apatosaurus, Stegosaurus, Ankylosaurus, Parasaurolophus, Gallimimus, Thecodontosaurus, Triceratops.

We look for the bones of dinosaurs.

We find them.

We dig them up.

We wrap them

and pack them.

We load them on trucks.

We have the bones of dinosaurs.

We have head bones, foot bones, leg bones,

rib bones, back bones, teeth and claws.

We put the claws on the foot bones

and the foot bones on the leg bones.

We put the teeth in the head bones

and the head bones on the neck bones.

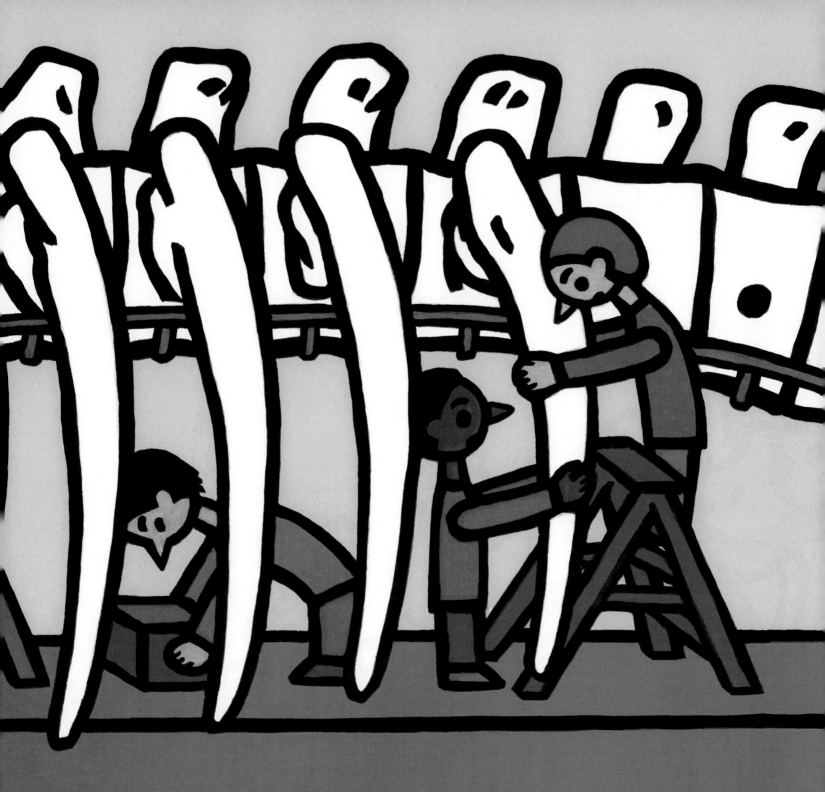

We put the rib bones on the back bones.

And the tail bones are last.

These are the bones of Tyrannosaurus rex.

Bones. Bones. We look for bones.
We look for the bones of dinosaurs.

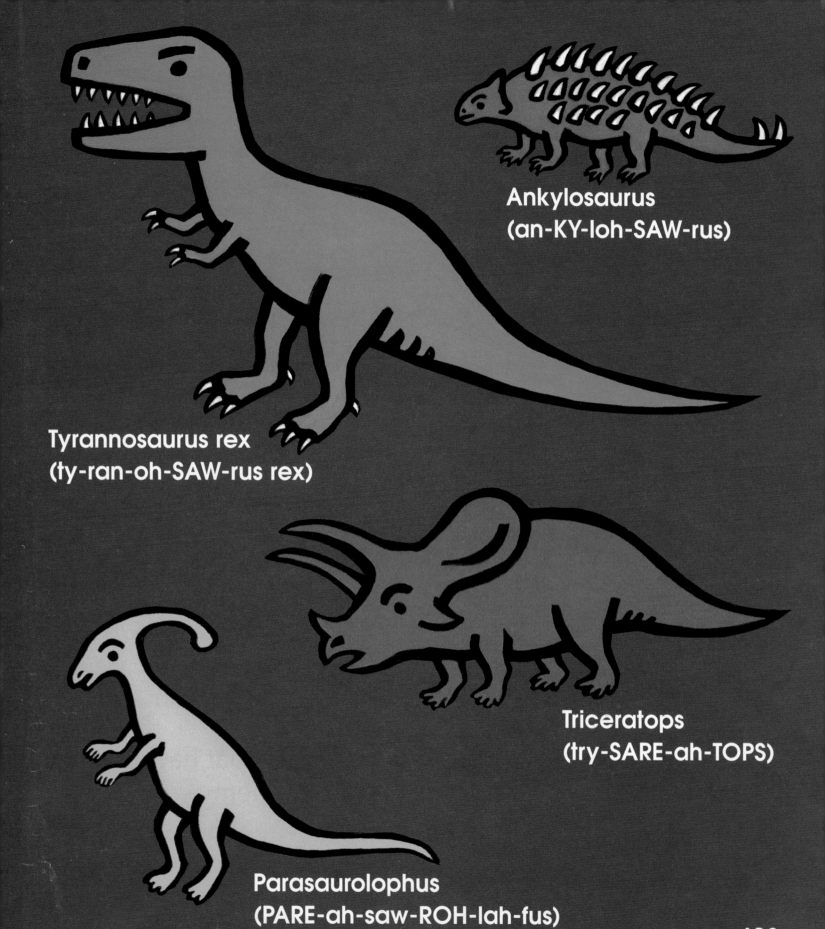

Ankylosaurus
(an-KY-loh-SAW-rus)

Tyrannosaurus rex
(ty-ran-oh-SAW-rus rex)

Triceratops
(try-SARE-ah-TOPS)

Parasaurolophus
(PARE-ah-saw-ROH-lah-fus)

139

Glossary

amazing
causing great surprise
The circus was **amazing.**

baby
a very
young child
A **baby** can't
walk or talk.

baby

basket
something used
to hold things
I put a **basket**
on my bicycle
handlebars.

basket

bet
a guess about who or what
will win
You can **bet** on who will
win a game, race, or contest.

bones
the hard parts of a person's
or animal's body under the
skin and muscles
There are 206 **bones** in the
human body.

candles
wax sticks that have strings
through them
Every year **candles** are put
on your birthday cake.

cat

a small animal that has soft fur, short ears, and a long tail

Many people like a **cat** as a pet.

cat

claws

the sharp nails on the feet of birds, dinosaurs, and many other animals

A dog uses its **claws** when it digs.

hole

an open place in something

There can be a **hole** in a roof, a sweater, or a street.

pocket

a place that holds small things

You can have a **pocket** in your shirt, pants, or skirt.

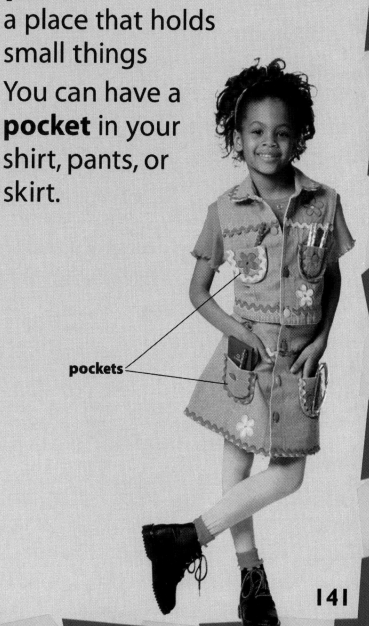

pockets

Authors and Illustrators

Byron Barton   pages 112–139

Byron Barton's favorite subjects in school were science, math, and art. When he grew up he went to art school. There he learned how to draw pictures of people and animals.

Before Byron Barton begins a new book, he reads and looks at pictures. Some other Byron Barton books are *Airport, Machines at Work,* and *Dinosaurs, Dinosaurs.*

Eric Carle   pages 40–63

Eric Carle's art is made in a very special way. He paints tissue paper with bright colors, then keeps the painted paper in drawers. When he is working on a story, he chooses just the right papers, then cuts and glues them to make the pictures he wants.

Eric Carle wants readers to have fun with his books. His most popular book is *The Very Hungry Caterpillar.*

Read Together!

Penny Dale   pages 64–89

Penny Dale gets many of her story ideas from things that happen to the children she knows. When her daughter Sarah was little, she did not always do what her mother asked. Then Penny Dale got an idea. She made up a game called "Bet You Can't!" Sarah then wanted to cooperate to show that she could! Another book by Penny Dale is *All About Alice*.

Taro Gomi   pages 10–21

Taro Gomi lives and works in Japan, but his books are read and enjoyed by children all over the world. He says, "I think a picture is words, and in my books I speak through my pictures."

Toot and *Where's the Fish?* are two other books by Taro Gomi that you can enjoy.

Acknowledgments

Grateful acknowledgment is made to the following sources for permission to reprint from previously published material. The publisher has made diligent efforts to trace the ownership of all copyrighted material in this volume and believes that all necessary permissions have been secured. If any errors or omissions have inadvertently been made, proper corrections will gladly be made in future editions.

Cover: Mike Reed.

Interior: "Who Hid It?" from WHO HID IT? by Taro Gomi. Copyright © 1991 by Taro Gomi. Reprinted by permission of The Millbrook Press Inc., Brookfield, CT.

"There's a Hole in My Pocket" from THERE'S A HOLE IN MY POCKET by Akimi Gibson, illustrated by Jeni Bassett. Copyright © 1994 by Scholastic Inc.

"Have You Seen My Cat?" from HAVE YOU SEEN MY CAT? by Eric Carle. Copyright © 1987 by Eric Carle Corporation. Reprinted with permission of Simon & Schuster Books for Young Readers, Simon & Schuster Children's Publishing Division.

"Bet You Can't" from BET YOU CAN'T by Penny Dale. Copyright © 1988 by Penny Dale. Reprinted by permission of HarperCollins Publishers.

"This Tooth" from MORE SURPRISES by Lee Bennett Hopkins. Copyright © 1987 by Lee Bennett Hopkins. Reprinted by permission of HarperCollins Publishers. Cover and illustration from TALKING LIKE THE RAIN, selected by X. J. Kennedy and Dorothy Kennedy, illustrated by Jane Dyer. Illustrations copyright © 1992 by Jane Dyer. Reprinted by permission of Little, Brown and Company.

"What's Inside?" from WHAT'S INSIDE? by Mary Jane Martin. Copyright © 1994 by Scholastic Inc.

"Baby Chick" from ALWAYS WONDERING by Aileen Fisher. Copyright © 1991 by Aileen Fisher.

Reprinted by permission of the author, who controls rights. SuperScience® Red is a registered trademark of Scholastic Inc. Logo used by permission.

"Bones, Bones, Dinosaur Bones" from BONES, BONES, DINOSAUR BONES by Byron Barton. Copyright © 1990 by Byron Barton. Reprinted by permission of HarperCollins Publishers.

Cover from ACROSS THE STREAM by Mirra Ginsburg, illustrated by Nancy Tafuri. Illustration copyright © 1982 by Nancy Tafuri. Published by William Morrow & Company, Inc.

Cover from I NEED A LUNCH BOX by Jeannette Caines, illustrated by Pat Cummings. Illustration copyright © 1988 by Pat Cummings. Published by HarperCollins Children's Books, a division of HarperCollins Publishers.

Cover from IS IT DARK? IS IT LIGHT? by Mary D. Lankford, illustrated by Stacey Schuett. Illustration copyright © 1991 by Stacey Schuett. Published by Alfred A. Knopf, Inc.

Cover from IT BEGINS WITH AN A by Stephanie Calmenson, illustrated by Marisabina Russo. Illustration copyright © 1993 by Marisabina Russo. Published by Hyperion Books for Children.

Cover from THE LITTLE MOUSE, THE RED RIPE STRAWBERRY, AND THE BIG HUNGRY BEAR by Don and Audrey Wood, illustrated by Don Wood. Copyright © 1984 by M. Twinn. Published by Child's Play (International) Ltd.

Photography and Illustration Credits

Selection Opener Photographs by David S. Waitz Photography/Alleycat Design, Inc.

Photos: p. 2 bl cat: © Russ Kinne/Comstock Inc.; cow: © Eric Neurath/Picture Perfect. pp. 2-3 pig: © Russ Kinne/Comstock Inc. p. 3 br: © Jim Heemstra for Scholastic Inc.; rooster: © Jack Elness/Comstock. Inc. p. 55 tr, bc: © Lawrence Migdale. pp. 94-95 Vittetoe (3): © Jim Heemstra for Scholastic Inc. p. 96 c: © Alan Black/ Bruce Coleman, Inc. p. 97 c: © G.I. Bernard/Animals Animals/Earth Scenes. p. 98 c: © S. J. Kraseman/Peter Arnold, Inc. p. 99 c: © E. R. Degginger/Photo Researchers, Inc. p. 100 c: © Zig Leszczynski/Animals Animals/Earth Scenes. p. 101 c: © Laura Riley/Bruce Coleman, Inc. p. 102 c: © Robert W. Hernandez/Photo Researchers, Inc. pp. 103-104: © Dwight Kuhn. pp. 105-106: © J. H. Robinson/Photo Researchers, Inc. p. 107 c: © C. C. Lockwood/Animals Animals/Earth Scenes. p. 108 c: © G. R. Zahn/Bruce Coleman, Inc. pp. 109: © E. R. Degginger/Animals Animals/ Earth Scenes. p. 110 c: © E. R. Degginger/Photo Researchers, Inc. p. 111: Eggs © Tom McHugh/ Photo Researchers, Inc.; Chick © Kelvin Aitken/Peter Arnold, Inc. p. 140 bl: © Michael Thompson/Comstock, Inc.; cl: © Anne Nielson/ Gamma Liason. p. 141 cl: © Steven W. Jones/ FPG International Corp.; br: Stephen Ogilvy for Scholastic Inc. p. 142 br: © Sigrid Estrada; bl: courtesy HarperCollins Children's Books. p. 143 bl: © Walker Books Ltd.

Illustrations: pp. 2-3: Jackie Snider; pp. 8-9: Jeannie Winston; p. 37: Jennifer Hewitson; pp. 38-39: Jeannie Winston; p. 51: Bradford Brown; p. 69: Jennifer Hewitson; pp. 90-91: Jane Dyer; pp. 92-93: Jeannie Winston.

DATE DUE